On Rudolf Steiner's MYSTERY DRAMAS

On Rudolf Steiner's MYSTERY DRAMAS

Four lectures
by
Ehrenfried Pfeiffer

Presented in Spring Valley
November 14, 28 and December 12, 26, 1948

MERCURY PRESS

On Rudolf Steiner's Mystery Dramas consists of notes on four lectures not revised by the lecturer and edited by Gerald F. Karnow, M.D.

Cover design by Kitsy McHenry,
Mystery Drama seals by Rudolf Steiner

ISBN: 978-1-957569-36-9

MERCURY PRESS
an imprint of SteinerBooks
834 Main Street, PO Box 358
Spencertown, New York 12165
www.steinerbooks.org

Contents

Lecture I
November 14, 1948

The consideration of the Mystery Plays probably belongs to one of the most intimate studies of anthroposophy. They explain in an artistic way what Rudolf Steiner gave in other places in terms of thought. Also, it seems to me that the plays are a continuation of Dr. Steiner's esoteric teachings as started in *Knowledge of Higher Worlds. Knowledge of Higher Worlds* describes the path to the awakening of the inner organs of perception.

Dr. Steiner said of *The Philosophy of Spiritual Activity*, *Knowledge of Higher Worlds*, *Theosophy*, *Occult Science*, and *The Spiritual Guidance of Mankind*, that if these books are carefully studied, one will find all the spiritual information given in any other of his books and any of his lectures. This is a big order.

The question has been raised: Why did Dr. Steiner never write a continuation of *Knowledge of Higher Worlds*? Actually, he did, but only in a way that one with eyes to see and ears to hear can discover. It is my experience that the four Mystery Plays are a sequel to *Knowledge of Higher Worlds*. So it is interesting to take these plays and read them from the point of view of a certain teaching. In contrast to *The Egyptian Book of the Dead*, they represent "The Book of Life." It is a story of human beings who find themselves in karmic connection, and try to get knowledge of higher worlds and bring it into practical life.

It becomes necessary to study each individual to see how they are influenced by Lucifer and Ahriman and by the guidance of their spiritual teacher. This is a long job. But I want to start today with some of the characters easiest to understand. The basic teaching of the plays is that they tell about karma and its working between human beings who have devoted themselves to study, and they show how this karma affects daily life.

I am using the method of looking backward, starting with the last play, *The Soul's Awakening*, first. For study I would suggest that you read the last play first, then *The Guardian of the Threshold*, etc. We read the fourth play to see how the characters have developed. Then we look back to the previous ones to see how they did it. We look at their development and we look at the hindering forces , the forces holding back the development of spiritual capacity. In the fourth play, you feel how it all goes wrong. It does not have a happy end; it is a tragic play. It does not have a solution, but that is the way life is. And we see what caused the difficulties.

These "books of life" are also instruction in how to behave. I have found in the past, in the life of the Society, that in cases of doubt as to how to decide, how to take other human beings, I would find answers if I looked at a situation in the *Mystery Plays* like the one I had encountered. There is a deeper, better value in this than the Romans found when they looked at the *Sybilline Books* before making a decision. The *Sybilline Books* were prophesies, out of a mind which was never able to achieve a clear, conscious, clairvoyant intuition, yet which told of spiritual forces. In these plays there are no prophecies, but actual events which we can use as a means for orienting our self to the events of our own life. We will not always find an answer, yet we can see how human beings speak out in a situation. It can help us to check up on our own thoughts, emotions, and will impulses, to check up on the good and the evil forces at work in own soul. It is interesting to compare these plays with our own anthroposophical life, but it would be wrong to try to find out who is who. It would be entirely wrong to find out who Benedictus was in the Anthroposophical Society, who Maria, Johannes, etc., was. The plays are not a "key novel"; they tell events objectively. Whether this or that one is the same personality is not important; rather, the structure and dynamics of the happenings is important.

The spiritual leader of the group is Benedictus. In all four plays, he conducts the spiritual development of the group members. In the first three, Benedictus is the spiritual leader, but at a distance from the physical affairs of his pupils. He is way above them, not linked with their personal fate. In the fourth play, Benedictus is now personally involved with the karma of his pupils, he enters into the business of his pupils. The fourth play was written by Dr. Steiner before the First World War. Regarding Benedictus, Dr. Steiner said in *The Soul's Awakening*, Benedictus is not only thought of as standing above his pupils, but interwoven with the soul fate, with the experience of his pupils. When we read this, we are reminded of Dr. Steiner's own fate. For years he stood above his pupils. Only shortly before his death, did he connect his own fate with that of his students. Despite such a parallel, it is not right to identify Rudolf Steiner with Benedictus.

Rather, we can see that in the fate of every spiritual teacher there comes a time when one cannot only teach but also make oneself manifest in a working group with one's pupils. And unless such a step is taken, the teacher remains abstract, and one's teachings do not take on eternal values. This is so because the task is that of transforming the earth, of bringing about mastership on earth. This cannot be done by teaching, but by doing with the hands. So the teacher then creates karma, one suffers and enjoys along with the others. And if such a group of human beings cooperates, they form a unit. They have their individual fate into which they are born as a result of previous lives; each has a tail like a comet. The tail makes the cooperation something that is not easy, it causes them to move in a wavering, in an erring line. Yet all these people want to find a unit. A unit is an organism of human beings, in the sense described by St. Paul in First Corinthians, 12—one body but many members. All are part of this organism. They form the eyes, ears, liver, heart, etc. They are individuals, but as far as the community is concerned, they form part of the unit. That is, in body and soul they have different functions, different tasks. These personalities have different impulses, different directions; they are not a unit yet. All that we have in the plays is on the one hand the spiritual guidance to bring about the existence of a unit, and on the other hand, the counter-forces trying to move this and that individual out of the unity. They deviate, then other forces work to bring them back. The spiritual leader works, and self recognition works, to bring you back to the mutual goal, which is to acknowledge the reality of the spirit, the recognition of the spirit. Also connected with our mutual goal is the fact that we feel Rudolf Steiner to be our leader and teacher. We have our personal karma so there are difficulties from the friction of personalities. Karma is the tail which we created and which we have to overcome. It causes friction, and sometimes makes us move in a wavering line. These are periods of (in Goethe's sense) analysis and of synthesis. Groups fall apart because they are not yet able to cooperate. It simply means that karma will bring them together later, until after a time they again have another fancy and go apart. This is the fate of the individual, of small groups and of large groups.

We have this cycle. If we take it as a reality, we see how the human group is brought together, splits apart again. It is together at the end in self recognition pointing to the future; but there is not a solution now, except complete absorption in the mutual goal of the recognition of the Spirit of Christ. If this completely penetrates all the members, then they are conscious parts of one organism. In nature, there is an organic whole, predetermined by the Creative Forces and carried out by their helpers, the Hierarchies. When an organism exists on the outer plane, the organism eventually dies, but the principle remains.

In the human realm, the human being is a whole in the self. Our task is first, recognition of the central force of the ego. Then develops the higher ego, which can recognize the ego in others; and together they can recognize spiritual leadership. The human being is a complete cosmic entity in the self. No forces shape it from without, only from within. This is because individuals are destined to develop freedom, and only out of freedom can unity come. The aim is to develop a new cosmos. Therefore in the old esoteric schools it was rightly said that the human being is the microcosm. Individuals have to develop their own sun, so that the other planets, the newly developed spiritual organs, can revolve around it.

Benedictus is the leader of this community. As soon as his karma is connected with that of the group, his teachings (they might be the best in the world) can only be manifest to the extent to which the pupils can absorb them. Benedictus is condemned by his own pupils, although he might be one of the highest initiates. His progress takes place only to the extent to which the smallest and most incomplete of his pupils is able to progress. This is a spiritual law. It is a common earthly fact that the progress of a factory or a farm is determined not by the fastest but by the slowest worker. This is also the fact in a spiritual community. The progress of the leader is determined by the speed of the development of the other beings in the group. We can see here that if one person is slow in the unit, either it will burst apart or the fastest will revolve in one spot until the slowest catches up. In the physical organism, if the heart works too fast, the blood in the foot is not able to follow, the foot is cold, or even necrosis may set in, while the heart has a fever—the whole is in disorder. So in the community, Benedictus has to keep step with the other organs that make it up.

In the fourth play we have the personality of Strader. He is the one who, because of taking some wrong paths in the past, is always endangered by Ahriman; yet he always has the knowledge by which he is able to overcome Ahriman. Thomasius unfortunately enters the Lucifer sphere. Lucifer has quite a hold on him, despite the work of Benedictus. Thomasius enters the Lucifer field. Strader has a task, but, because the others do not cooperate, are lost in their own problems, Strader makes a mistake. The community is so hurt by Thomasius' mistake and Strader's inability to act, that fate knows no answer except that Strader dies. The others become introverted as he is extroverted. The community is maintained by Strader's being put onto another planet for a time. His sacrifice maintains the community. In our solar system, the sun has the most intense combustion, the earth could not stand it. So the sun separated from the earth.

The physical situation of the fourth play is that a group of people have formed themselves to build a business. They have a sawmill and carpenter shop. Quite a few members of the group are in the enterprise. So far they have been doing good work, creating a firm with a good name. But the owner, Hilary, has contacts with Benedictus, and with spiritual experiences. In spite of the fact that Hilary is a good business man, he has spiritual inclinations. He has a kind of clairvoyance, so that he sees a lot of spiritual powers. But he is not a master yet of the physical or spiritual situation.

He has decided to introduce spiritual impulses into his business. We ourselves may have decided to introduce anthroposophy into our business, our factories or our farms—and what happens? We see what happens in the play. Hilary, out of faithfulness to Benedictus, feels him to be a spiritual leader, and feels that certain of Benedictus' pupils would give his cabinetmaking business a new impulse. He decides, for example, that instead of square houses and rectangular chairs, he will introduce artistic forms. He thinks that Thomasius might be able to make the designs and patterns for these.

There are practical men in the firm, who have helped Hilary for years with their common sense. These men now have complaints. As the play starts, the secretary and the manager complain that the clients are dissatisfied, that they think the quality of the work and the firm's punctuality are declining.

In our anthropological enterprises, we have had something into which we have tried to introduce an anthroposophical idea. I agree with the manager and the secretary that we generally find the quality declining and the punctuality weakening. Today, in an ordinary business, we would in such a case either have to give up or to fire the people. But in a community based on spiritual laws, we would have to fight and stick it out.

Hilary, in addition, wants to introduce something entirely new. Strader, in his studies, has discovered a nature force previously not known. Strader constructs an apparatus to collect hitherto unknown cosmic rays or cosmic energy. Then he makes an apparatus to transform vibrations of high amplitude and low force into low amplitude and high force. Dr. Steiner said the idea was of a motor by means of which everyone, in their own home, could produce warmth, heat and light. Such a device would completely revolutionize our present social concepts; it would free us from material cares and bring about a new social structure. It would mean a complete decentralization of industry. All this was in the concept of Strader, as we learn from Dr. Steiner.

In the last century there was a similar approach in Philadelphia. A man named Keeley built a machine which used radiations of the human body and exerted a pressure of 40,000 pounds per square inch. He failed, because others wanted to use it in a selfish way. The idea perished; the motor is still on a junk pile in Philadelphia. Also, I believe he failed because the idea was entirely premature at his time. It is also the inspiration of Ahriman. We have drawings of Strader's machine, but it cannot work, because there is an error in it. People are not able to correct the error, because we are not spiritually advanced enough.

It is an interesting situation in the play. We can study how they behaved, because we have similar problems today and can learn from it. In the first scene, we are in the office of Hilary, with the secretary and manager. Hilary is told that some of the customers are dissatisfied. The manager tells him that the punctuality of the firm is declining, and its good name is suffering. It is an old-fashioned business, probably managed in a patriarchal way. Dr. Steiner's stage directions say the office is furnished in a not-too-modern style.

I would like to insert parenthetically, regarding the reading of the plays: Once long ago when I read *The Philosophy of Spiritual Activity* I started to underline what I considered important. After some time I discovered that every line was underlined. One can make a similar discovery regarding the Mystery Plays. Probably the reason that some people, on reading the plays or attending the Dornach performances, get so tired is because that everything in the plays has 100% value. There is nothing you can skip.

That his is an old-fashioned firm is important in regard to the understanding of Hilary. Hilary represents traditional spiritual science, inclined to what has been brought from the past. Out of this we understand his difficulty in building up an adequate institution for Strader, and also his problems connected with the accepting of Thomasius. He overestimates and underestimates values. Hilary is able to finance the venture, but because of his weakness nothing comes out of it.

I have tried to construct a "time-table," following each character through the plays, to see what they have done in the physical or spiritual world, and to see how they coincide or disagree with one another. Hilary is one of the most interesting characters in the Mystery Plays. He is important because all of Benedictus' wants are financed by him, and also because of his tremendous spiritual background. Hilary, in the past, has always been connected with occultism. He was Grand Master of a mystical order in Medieval times, and a successor of Benedictus in this position. This indicates that he was quite a personality then. And in the Egyptian Mysteries he was Keeper of the Magic Word by which the Portal of Death was opened or closed—quite a responsible position. Then according to his occult development, he became successor to Benedictus as Grand Master in the Medieval Castle in Austria on the Austro-Hungarian border, in the Burgenland. In my book, *The Earth's Face* there is a picture showing a traditional landscape with a castle. Dr. Steiner confirmed that this is the place where the order used to live. Here Hilary said that he wanted to plant germs for the future before they perish. Then there was a peasant revolt and a disagreement with the Church; the Grand Master feels that it will be necessary to develop into a higher spiritual life through pain and error. The effort of the Mystical Brotherhood in the Middle Ages was a failure and had to perish. Hilary as Grand Master understood that this failure was because the inner enemy in man withstands the aim of forming one brotherhood.

We understand Hilary's desire to maintain an occult order, because of his active and responsible role in the Egyptian period. This left an impulse to work for such a spiritual community as existed in the Egyptian Mysteries. His impulse is to bring people to form a brotherhood; he wanted to do this in a lumber business in connection with spiritual guidance. In the third play we find Hilary telling the history of the Mystical

Order and saying that it is time to reveal the content of the spirit to all people. In the Middle Ages it went wrong; the time was just not ripe. Now he thinks again that this impulse can be brought to fruition. But hearing the reaction of the listeners, he again concludes that the time is not yet ripe for action. The people who should cooperate do not want to do so yet.

He prepares Thomasius for the task of the artistic leadership of the business. But Hilary, though he is a great personality, makes a very typical mistake. He is a representative of traditional methods of occultism, and wants to maintain something that was right in the Egyptian Period into our period, where it is wrong. This is a Luciferic impulse, and is the mistake of the Catholic Church.

On the other hand, while it is right to give Spiritual Science to all, it is premature to do so if one does not find people to accept it. This is the Ahrimanic deception. Hilary in the Egyptian time was Keeper of the Word. In the Middle Ages he was the Grand Master. Today he heads a business. He is a little better than a Freemason. He wants to bring the spirit to all men, and to make the spirit a reality on earth. But the time is not ripe. The time of the traditional occultism has expired, and the people are not ready for the new. So the decision to bring spiritual knowledge is made too soon. That is, it is an Ahrimanic decision: it is too early, the time is not yet ripe. It is like picking an artificially ripened fruit.

In the eighth scene of *The Guardian of the Threshold*, Hilary goes into the realm of Ahriman with companions—this is thirteen years before the last play. He says he thinks that Ahriman's realm is good. This is the great deception suffered by all past orders brought into the present. They say that Ahriman is bad, but act as if he were good. Hilary makes two mistakes: one is preserving traditional occultism, the other is bringing a correct thing too early.

At the end of the fourth play he is disturbed. He says: On what can we rely when nothing holds? He feels that he wants to do something out of the old traditional spirituality, which has expired. At the same time, the new is not living in him yet as a life practice. He feels loneliness of soul. He can look into the spiritual world, but he cannot interpret what he sees. He draws the only right conclusion under the circumstances: he decides to wait until the spirit will show him the way. The only thing to do with that which we desire is to hold it back so that it will mature. This is one teaching from the plays which we can gather for the spiritual world so far: if we recognize that we are doing something which belongs to the past or which anticipates the future, we will decide to wait until the spirit tells us. If you do this, then you will do right.

Lecture II
November 28, 1948

A brief summary of the last lecture may be helpful to those who were not here last time. These plays may be experienced in two ways; first, we may read them, or see a performance of them, and have an artistic experience; second, we may experience them as a dramatic performance of the Mysteries. Considering them in the second fashion, we will find that the meaning, and our understanding of it, goes deeper. Having read them often, and seen every performance at Dornach during a period of ten years, I have felt that I would like to call them the "Book of Life," in contrast with the Egyptian Mysteries' *The Book of the Dead.* The latter is an experience of the human soul after death when it returns to the realm of Isis and Osiris. The Mystery Plays tell us of the outer and inner experiences of a group of people connected through several incarnations and acting out spiritual impulses.

They show us the inner experiences of the group, individuals whose development comes in conflict with the inner development of others, with the karma of the group, and outer circumstances. In the way of life itself, we find that in the plays there will be beautiful experiences and there will be conflicts. The conflicts will only be solved if we understand them and solve them out of understanding. Many conflicts are not solved until we find a higher degree of understanding. So this advancement to a higher degree, and who advances, is important in the Mystery Plays. The last play, *The Soul's Awakening,* does not close with a happy ending. It closes with a lot of conflicts still unsolved, so it is true to life.

The plays can be grouped as the first two and the last two. The first two were written by Rudolf Steiner on the inspiration of a human being who was devoted to him and had intended to write such plays but died before she could accomplish this. She inspired him to write the first and second play out of the spiritual world. He signed the first two plays "Through Rudolf Steiner" and the last two "By Rudolf Steiner." In the latter two he carried on the work no longer inspired by this individual.

We have personalities in the plays connected with different appearances of the spirit in the soul life. There is one group which is more the bearer of the will impulse. Another represents the essence of spiritual life. A third group represents soul life, the metamorphosis of the spirit in the soul element. Humans in these groups represent pure soul forces, or pure will forces, or other forces, along with their own individual impulses. There are also twelve representing every-day human life, who belong to the community of the play. They are not so important. When these twelve appear, Ahriman says a thirteenth would again be like the first. There are twelve types of human beings, but we must not forget this—it is Ahriman's idea to classify them.

The Mystery Plays lead us into a situation where one part of the actors is immersed in outer life and tries to develop spiritual life, and another group, which has been the bearer of a spiritual impulse, in an occult brotherhood, is trying to bring the inner life to the outer world. So the interpenetration of the inner and the outer is portrayed.

I started with the fourth play, and will continue in a kind of looking backward, so that we can see the characters in the earlier plays. This gives us the possibility of seeing how many events of a present situation are the results of a past one, and of seeing what can be improved in an individual and what belongs to the eternal entelechy and to the future. I feel that the Mystery Plays can be consulted in every decision of our personal life. If we get stuck in relation to other beings, including Lucifer and Ahriman, we can look up the corresponding situation in the plays, as an example of our own inner decision. We can read them as a continuation of Dr. Steiner's *Knowledge of Higher Worlds* and the first steps shown in that book.

Today we will continue with *The Soul's Awakening.* A group has started a business undertaking on earth. Hilary is the owner of a woodworking and furniture company. It has been a successful, well-established concern, inherited from his ancestors. It was a traditionally developed enterprise. At the same time, Hilary had been an outstanding personality in the Mystical Brotherhood, and felt that it was time to bring forth the impulses developed in the brotherhood by its leader. Nowadays, we also have occult brotherhoods, for example the Freemasons. But these people do not try to practice their occultism in their daily work. They use a kind of double bookkeeping. Hilary has taken the next step; he tries to bring together the spiritual impulse and the business impulse—and right away there is trouble. When he tries to introduce Thomasius, to help the manufacturing in an artistic way, there is trouble; when he tries to introduce Strader, to make use of a new mechanical force of nature, there is trouble again. This is because their personal karma and their and their individual degree of maturity and imperfections influence the daily outer activity. If we read the plays carefully, we see that these things can't be avoided, they happen and must be fought through. The solution can only be found if people inwardly find the solution. The inner development affects the outer.

What I mean can be seen by reading the Plays. They can be read for their abstract intellectual content. Then they will remain as thoughts, and finally we will judge them on the basis of sympathy or antipathy. On the other hand, we can read any book in such a way that we re-create it, as active beings and personalities: we add the substance and understanding of our own soul so as to make it alive. If we do that, then these figures become realities.

Dr. Steiner once said regarding Shakespeare, that his figures were actually *living* figures, they have their own life, their karma and incarnations, although they were created from Shakespeare's fantasy. This can also be observed in regard to Goethe's *Faust*, which describes an actual human being. The Mystery Plays are like these, and the best way to see the characters in them as personalities is to read the plays to oneself aloud. One need not use "speech formation," but the reading aloud, the action of this, will bring them to life.

It is good to read one role at a time, as if you were that person yourself. At one time read Strader, as though you were Strader, another time, Thomasius, Blade, even Lucifer and Ahriman. Then you feel them alive, friends or enemies of yours.

We have to marvel if we consider the way these plays were written. Dr. Steiner had no time to write the plays, between his travels and lectures. Frequently, when one of them was being given its first rehearsals, they would be working on one scene with the next not yet written. But he would do it overnight, and bring it the next day. They came out of his spiritual experience.

The personalities of the fourth play include representatives of the purely spiritual element, the devotional element and the will element. Benedictus and Hilary are representatives of the spiritual element. In Benedictus is represented a spiritual leader who shows up as such all the way through. Hilary is also a leading representative of the spiritual element, particularly of the traditional spiritual. In Egypt, he was the recorder, in the medieval scenes he was Grand Master of the Knights. In the third play, he was Grand Master of the Brotherhood. The impulse in his entelechy is to go along with traditional elements, in occultism and in his business. So it is a step forward and he tries to incorporate new spiritual influences into the traditional. As such, the attempt is admirable; but it is a tragedy, because everything he tries is a failure.

Hilary is a typical American businessman. All he wants to do is to organize. And he wants to try to combine spiritual and business life. When he tried to introduce new artistic forces and new natural forces, the trouble started. His clients complained about a decline in quality of the goods and punctuality. Old employees bring forward practical common sense as an argument against what Hilary is trying to do. There is an example from practical life: if an anthroposophist starts a business venture, let us say a bio-dynamic farm or garden, he does it primarily because he is an anthroposophist. He employs anthroposophists and non-anthroposophists. He has to make the latter also understand his ideas. And he has to *listen* to what, for example, an old experienced ploughman has to tell him. Gradually both points of view have to blend.

Such a practical man is Hilary's secretary, Frederick Clearmind. He is a practical man, but he has not obtained spiritual knowledge, so unconsciously he is used by Ahriman, that spirit who denies the good and yet helps the good. Ahriman is not interested in human beings who want to build bridges from the spiritual to the physical, and embody spiritual impulses in the physical. He tries to hinder them, because he is the spirit who makes matter dense and hard, so that we take it to be *the* reality, instead of a special, transitory form of energy. As long as we believe only in matter, we are inspired by Ahriman. So Ahriman does not like Hilary's attempt, and tries to disturb it. Ahriman's way of disturbing an idea is to cause doubts, especially in scientifically-minded people. So we see personalities like the secretary, and others, who cast doubt on the project, doubts founded on very good arguments. He casts doubts also into people devoted to the soul element, but here the doubts are more as to their own experiences. This is particularly true of Strader, who is the "hero" of the fourth play. When Strader achieves his goal, his initiation, he meets no one who understands him fully or is able to continue what he started. So Strader has to die. Dr. Steiner said it was Strader's karma not to go on, because he was left entirely alone.

Strader had developed a machine to transform cosmic radiations into vibrations used mechanically. Dr. Steiner gave drawings for a machine to be built as a model for use on the stage. Some anthroposophists made the mistake of thinking it could be constructed as an actual machine. It would never work, because it contains an error imposed by Ahriman. Dr. Steiner said that the idea was for every household to have a small model of the Strader machine, for producing light, heat, and mechanical energy needed. The way Strader intended the machine, its mechanical problem was not solvable. He learned, at the end, what was wrong with the machine; and in that moment he died, because the situation was not ready for it.

I once asked Dr. Steiner about the possible use of etheric forces. He made certain suggestions for experiments to be done to see whether a suitable machine could be constructed. The results were negative. When I told him this, he said, it is an answer from the spiritual world. It shows that the time is not yet ripe for it. Such a machine, he continued, could only succeed when the Threefold Order had been manifested on earth; the experiment should not be tried before that.

It is interesting to follow up Strader to see how the error slipped into his insight and disturbed both his mechanical perception and his relationship to others in the group. Strader, in the beginning, was an entirely materialistic scientist, with not much faith in the spirit. Then he met a situation that overthrew his materialistic concepts.

The prototype of Strader actually had been forced by his foster parents to live in a Capucin Monastery in Dornach,

Switzerland in his youth. At that time, the Goetheanum did not yet exist. The monastery was a small one, with only twenty to thirty monks. He broke loose from this place because he had an intellectual, scientific, investigating type of mind. Dr. Steiner said that this prototype of Strader was a man named Gideon Spicker, who lived in the middle and end of the nineteenth century and died in twentieth century, at about the time Strader died in the Mystery Plays. It is difficult to establish the relationship between Gideon Spicker and Strader, but Spicker broke loose from the Capucins and became a philosophy professor in a German town. I once read his book, a materialistic philosophy concerning God. It was most abstract. But it is interesting that in this personality lived something that tried to extend into deeper knowledge of nature and God. According to his personality he was an initiate, but in this life, because of earlier mistakes, he could not act out of initiate consciousness.

Dr. Steiner said there were many natural scientists today who had been Egyptian initiates. They are today unsatisfactory to themselves, and experience inner doubt; they are tragic figures. We can see how Ahriman tries to disturb our mind, especially if we are scientifically minded. In Egypt, Strader was Impersonator of the Fire Element, the Mysteries of Vulcan. These are connected with our will power, and the task of transforming the earth. Prometheus was an initiate of Vulcan. All that is described to us as modern science derives from the Vulcan Mysteries.

We can follow Strader back to the Atlantean Time, when he was already connected with the Mystery of Vulcan. He played a role as representative of natural force, not yet a fully awakened human being. His human ego was subdued. He was not yet a full-fledged initiate. But in the Egyptian Time he was advanced enough to impersonate a Nature Element, not fully human yet. In Medieval Times he was the persecuted

Jew; through his Egyptian impersonation of the fire element, he received a deep insight into Nature. So it was his destiny to become a natural scientist. And he brought with him a very strong intellectual power. He can think, because thought is the same power which brings about the arrangements in Nature. But through his sufferings as Simon the Jew he had developed a *very* sensitive soul.

There is a danger facing all who have gone through the Mysteries of Vulcan: Ahriman tries to get and hold them, because he knows as much about nature as they do, and vice versa. They, if interpenetrated with the Christ Impulse, are just the ones who can counteract Ahriman. Unfortunately, Spicker had committed a serious sin in his medieval incarnation. He was a singer taking part in the Saengerkrieg at the Wartburg, and tried to give the best possible performance. His opponent was Wolfram von Eschenbach, whose songs were filled with the inner soul of the Grail Impulse (out of the Buddhist stream). Spicker, who was Heinrich von Ofterdingen, did not have behind him the impulse of the Mystical Grail, and he felt he would lose in the contest because he could only sing out of his intellect and natural forces. So he called the elements to help, and used magical powers to call the Leader of the Elements, Klingsor the Sorcerer, who was willing to influence the physical events as a sorcerer. Whoever is of the true spiritual stream never uses spiritual power for physical wants. (In most recent times Blavatsky made teacups appear and disappear, misusing spiritual powers.)

So Heinrich von Ofterdingen called on the leader of the magical elements, Klingsor the Sorcerer, to help him win his contest. He yielded his individuality and became a bearer of Klingsor forces. This created karmic guilt, with the result that in his next life he was not able to make immediate contact with the spiritual world, but started as a materialistic scientist. But things had happened in between which balanced out the Klingsor guilt. He was not a complete Klingsor follower. Yet in his Strader life, nothing that he does is he able to bring to completion. He is always hindered. This is due to the fact that at one time he yielded to wrong occult forces. For instance, in *The Soul's Probation,* he met Theodora. Theodora is really the pure soul with no dark forces having a hold over it. It is not intellectual, but a simple soul so purified that it almost borders on the nature of an angel being. Theodora is clairvoyant, not because of initiation but because she is so pure that insight into the spirit is given to her. She is a true seeress. In conscious visions, as all her visions were, she announced the coming of the Etheric Christ. Strader was present at such a time, and felt it to be the turning point of his life, with all the past forces thrown out. And reflecting as a scientist, he spoke of the nothingness of our own thinking. He felt that at the moment of facing the highest, exact science strives in vain.

Strader had met some queer people in this group of searchers for the Spirit. Thomasius, admired as an artist, had the fate that always when he had a fine idea he would fall into the arms of Lucifer. Thomasius had been destined to become the teacher of the spiritual movement inspired by Benedictus, to talk about Benedictus's spiritual science. But he always fell for Lucifer. Strader, seeing things as Thomasius saw them, got the shock of his life. He couldn't accept spiritual science, and almost lost his own mind. The result was that he was mentally sick for a long time. The study of nature brought him back to reason. This was possible because of his own karmic beginnings. Then he decided to avoid all further searching—to recover his self first. (This can be good advice for others.) He gave up scientific research and spiritual investigation to find his inner entelechy before going ahead on the path. He entered a machine shop as manager. The karma of nothingness balanced his guilt as Heinrich von Ofterdingen.

He amazed Capesius by speaking this time of reincarnation. But Strader knows that he would be able to continue a worthy spiritual life. For many years he went on in this inner pain and uncertainty; he even yielded to darkness. The more we look at the person of Strader, we see the modern human being in the scientific world. It is a yielding to darkness and blending into a future spiritual stream. Many, such as De Nouys, Lindbergh, and St. Exupery have met the spirit at similar thresholds. Some die, like St. Exupery; De Nouys became a Catholic. Strader fights on. Across the threshold is Strader, as a beacon to those who have to undergo a similar fate.

Lecture III
December 12, 1948

Probably the main figure in the Mystery Dramas (in fact Dr. Steiner said he was the main figure) is Johannes Thomasius. Johannes Thomasius is on the borderline of the threshold of the Spiritual World. He is an artist, and according to kara, he is destined to be a teacher of spiritual science. He is at a point where the ordinary physical concept changes to a spiritual concept, and he goes through the struggles of one who loses the basis of the physical concept and tries to develop a spiritual one.

So it is the fate of Johannes Thomasius which, in a way, determines the fate of the entire group that constitutes the cast of the play. The group is connected through a mutual karma. Most of them have in their karma something that directs them to spiritual science. They also, in their earthly karma, have hindrances; and their entire karma is so interlocked that if *one succeeds*, it helps the whole group and if *one fails* the whole group is handicapped.

We see in the plays several fresh attempts to bring spiritual science to humanity: one in the Middle Ages, one in Egypt, and two attempts in our present time. These trials, I am sorry to say, do not succeed. I cannot say they fail, because in spiritual science there is no failure, but lack of success and postponement. In the Middle Ages, the antagonism between the Catholic Group and Rosicrucian Knights is so strong that no peace can be brought about. There is need of a postponement in order to bring spiritual science to the uninitiated.

We see how in the present the mystical society again attempts to present insight to the uninitiated. And those who were antagonists in medieval times are now willing to listen, although not to accept. But there is one step forward in the relations of the Catholic and Mystical groups, if we see the change in the relationship between Maria and Johannes Thomasius, as compared with that between the Monk and Thomas the Miner.

There is one person who stands above the fate of all the others until, in the last play, he unites his life and fate with that of the group. This is Benedictus. What this means, we see in the last play in which Johannes Thomasius falls into the hands of Lucifer, and therefore the others are more exposed to Ahrimanic forces. The result is that even the power of vision of Benedictus is dimmed for a moment. He is able to escape the binding forces; in his thinking he can repel Ahriman, but still his own task is impaired. It is perhaps the most important lesson of the Plays, that a spiritual leader and his pupils are so connected that if the pupils do not achieve their task he is unable to complete his mission.

We can apply this to Rudolf Steiner. The fact that in the Anthroposophical Society his pupils have not achieved their aims, has cast a shadow on Rudolf Steiner's mission. This we should keep in mind regarding our own spiritual life, and the spiritual life of our community—the Anthroposophical Society. We should remember that no honors are gained by insisting upon our own thinking. This is perishable. We foster the movement by spiritual achievements made through hard labor, not through insisting upon our own opinions, even though our own opinions are based on inner consciousness.

We ask ourselves: what is the character, what is the definition of a spiritual leader? If you read the plays 50 times, and study Benedictus, you come to a peculiar answer: This spiritual leader, except for one instance, never interferes with the physical life, the physical aims and endeavors of the group with which he is connected. He gives advice—not as to how the group should be organized or behave—he only advises regarding the inner development of the individual being. He advises a person how, on the inner path, one should learn to deepen the forces of cognition living in the self. This is important because it is a law of the spiritual world that a person who is initiated, who can cross the Threshold must—unless it is particularly demanded by the spiritual world—give only advice, only teaching, as to how to reach, and cross objectively, the Threshold of the Spirit. The initiate never interferes with personal karma, never says what the group should do in the physical world.

In the last play, everything is wrong. Yet Benedictus does not advise Hilary regarding his business plans, he does not tell Strader what is wrong with his machine, nor does he advise Thomasius regarding his artistic plans. But he does advise them regarding the crossing of the Threshold, he tells them how they can recognize Ahriman and Lucifer. He tells them of the karma that brought about a situation, and tells of the forces of soul that are needed to overcome a situation.

These are the characteristics of a spiritual leader. And if, out of study of what Rudolf Steiner has given, I were asked to determine whether a person is a spiritual leader, I would ask myself: Does he behave as Benedictus does in the Mystery Plays? Does he advise us how to perfect our own karma, how to meet Lucifer and Ahriman? If a person claiming spiritual leadership answers these questions positively, I would trust him. If he did not, I would feel that I could not trust him as a spiritual leader.

Guided by Rudolf Steiner, because I have the feeling that he has the deepest insight, I never would condemn you for your present incompleteness, but show you how to complete yourself more, teach you how to meditate, teach you how to recognize Lucifer and Ahriman. I would teach you to strengthen the deepest forces of your soul as represented by Philia, Astrid, and Luna, who correspond more or less to the Sentient Soul, Intellectual Soul, and Consciousness Soul. Rudolf Steiner outlines the task. He leaves you free as to how to fulfill it. If you do not fulfill it, he would say, this is also a necessity, we can metamorphose the plans. This is cooperation in complete freedom. I have not found such leadership as that of Rudolf Steiner since he crossed the Threshold of Death, and I must still recognize Rudolf Steiner as the only spiritual leader in our society.

It is only once that Benedictus tries to interfere with history. This is in the Medieval Scenes where Maria, as the Monk, enters the castle of the Brotherhood. The monk feels its atmosphere hostile to everything his education has taught him is good. At this moment, the monk is trying to take away the knights' foundation, their rights in the land. The ownership is not established. He says the Church is the sole owner, and therefore they ought to be deprived of their rights. This sounds very familiar to us. At this moment, Benedictus interferes, because if the situation were to continue it would make it impossible to unite the Brotherhood stream and the Monk stream in the next life; there would be no possibility of union.

Benedictus there interferes. He interferes as a spiritual being, not incarnated. He had died 50 years before. He appears out of the realms of the dead to the Monk (Maria). Spiritual beings can only interfere with physical work when they (the individual spiritual beings) are not in the body but outside, as purely spiritual agents. It is important to realize this, because again it throws a certain light on problems that concern us in our work as followers of Rudolf Steiner. It is so important that I would like to read from this scene.

(Here followed reading from the scene with the Second Preceptor. The lecturer noted, in passing, that the mines in question, now abandoned, still exist.)

In the moment in which the Monk thinks he has to summon his forces to defy "the enemy", Benedictus appears. We might ask ourselves, in a similar situation: Might it not be that what we, uninitiated, call "the enemy", could be the teacher himself wishing to speak with us? Then we would be listening instead of repelling.

Benedictus shows the monk that he is in error in attacking the Brotherhood, and in doing so on the basis of words he spoke while still on earth. He says his words should not be preserved as dogma, but rather that they are to be lived with, evolved in harmony with the needs of newer times. He tells the Monk to judge as he himself would if he were with him on earth at this later time. He interferes to help the Monk so that the Monk will not harm but understand and work towards peaceful union. His teaching was "Alone by peaceful union of the aims..."

Now a very important thing happens. At such moments, when decisive karma becomes manifest, when the preparation of the presenting of spiritual science is endangered, of course Lucifer and Ahriman will be very alert and will have their say too; because it is in their interest that such a peaceful union not be brought about. So they speak to the Monk and try to weaken the influence of Benedictus's spirit by bringing in doubt and fear. Here also Benedictus, true to the fashion of a spiritual leader, can only give advice and point to what ought to be, The Monk can heed or not heed, out of his own free will.

Ahriman says that the advice of Benedictus comes from another realm in which it might be correct, but if it is obeyed here it might lead to utter confusion. He tells the Monk to be guided only by his reason and senses. Ahriman calls what Benedictus says, regarding living in friendship with the other group, error. If you take this sentence separately, it sounds perfect. Ahriman is very clever. He influences us to see black as white and vice versa.

Lucifer also sounds like common sense. We hear every day that "we are living in changing times". But, he says, it is not for the heretics to trace the path, but only for the Catholic Concept. Catholic, comes from the Greek word, *Kat holen gaen*, meaning "ruling all over the world", in other words, the only accepted opinion, only your faith is the right one. Lucifer says the error is dangerous because it speaks the truth.

The Monk recognizes the conflicting voices and asks, how is he to find the path to good if the powers of evil are recommending it? He draws the only conclusion, the one that everyone should draw: "the wisdom of My Master shall reveal the meaning of his words". Imagine yourself as the monk, a faithful pupil of Benedictus, a faithful servant of the order he founded. You received a task from this Order, and your Spiritual Teacher says: Don't do it, and Ahriman and Lucifer tell you the words we have just read in the scene. It is not an easy struggle, it involves the life and death of your inner soul life. You can ask: How shall I find the path that leads to good? And Benedictus answers, I can direct you *if* you let my words on earth possess you and find the life in them here. He says: Walk the path towards the spiritual world, revive the words of the Master in your inmost soul, and the proper path will be made plain. That is, he is calling on the inmost powers of the Monk to cross the Threshold and enter recognition. All he can do is withdraw from physical action and develop spiritual self-recognition. He might have to give up physical action and go on the path of initiation first.

That is why, in connection with the struggles of our Society, a year ago I suggested a truce, because I felt that we should not act but follow the words of John the Baptist, "Repent, change your minds", go on the path first, where you meet your Teacher face to face. You can't do harm if you are constantly walking the path. Not by accident was this play called *The Soul's Probation.* This is the trial in which we and our society dwell at this moment. If we learn from the words of Benedictus, we will find the way to the realm where we will not destroy but leave the way open for union, for building up something which will bear fruit in the future.

Maria as the Monk, in her karma, seems to me to be a representative of the human being who develops the consciousness soul in a very modern way. Out of her consciousness soul, she helps to keep Thomasius from losing himself too far in Lucifer's realm. She tries to keep him on the path and help him to overcome Lucifer's temptation. She can do this because of what happened in the Egyptian Scenes (which took place in the time of the Eighteenth Dynasty). Until then, the human being had not entered the realm of freedom, which was guarded by the priest kings. The initiator formed imaginations or inspirations, so that the neophyte could see them in the temple of sleep. Then he wakened to spiritual consciousness. It was not done out of his own volition, he was put in an ecstatic state. It is interesting that modern Yoga and other esoteric schools maintain this feature of initiation. When asked: "Where can you find God?" the pupil answers: "In the heart of my guru." It is the guru's task to prepare himself so that the pupil sees God there in the form of a symbol or thought.

At a certain moment, this had to be interrupted. The initiator withheld his thoughts, his own imagination so that the pupil found a blank in the spiritual world and with non-initiate powers of soul he spoke into the world of initiation. And in this very moment was one of the decisive cornerstones in the history of humanity. The pupil passed the threshold out of his own lower consciousness. Everyone got excited, there was complete uproar, the sphinxes spoke, the old spiritual traditions had been interrupted. From one point of view this was a dreadful moment, a moment of spiritual crime. Yet this was the moment when the pupil could enter the spiritual world out of his own self, his own labor.

The moment had caused all the later misunderstanding, hatred and offense of one group against any other group, this moment of the birth of the ego through error. Only through error can we recognize truth. We have to walk the path of error. Maria did, and in the medieval times she offended the Brotherhood which had withheld initiation from her in Egypt. Benedictus saw that the only way she would be able in the future, fully conscious, to enter the spiritual world and be of use as a guide to other beings, was to go through this error and find the truth.

Lecture IV
December 26, 1948

The Shepherds and Kings came a long way to celebrate the birth of the Jesus Child. The Kings came from the East, with gold, myrrh and frankincense. The Kings represent the wisdom of the East, that wisdom related to the stars, to which in Egypt was called Isis, the cosmic wisdom. The Shepherds also came a long way, although this does not appear in the story. They "happened to be there" only because they had come a long distance.

The Jesus Child also had to come a long way in his development. According to Anthroposophy and Dr. Steiner's teaching, the Jesus Child composed himself out of the synthesis of two streams. One was the stream of initiation, of deep insight, which came through Zarathustra so that there would be such a body and soul able to take the Christ into it. The body of this Jesus Child was prepared from very ancient times. And also, we look in this Child, on Adam Kadmon, preserved in his original glory, not driven from Paradise. Only such a body could become the bearer of Christ, the Sun God. The Shepherds and the Kings were earthly beings, while in the Jesus Child there was combined the Divine and the most highly developed human being.

In the pattern of a spiritual impulse we can follow the Shepherds and the Kings into the past of human history and discern two streams of searchers for truth. The stream of the Kings was always called by this name in the history of the Mysteries. They have to do with the God-sent wisdom of Creation, the world of the stars, the zodiac, sun, moon and the planets—that which, from without, formed the world according to creative *thought*. On the other side are the Shepherds—here there is no philosophic thought but perceptive *feeling*—there are simple humble men who through a refined inner life are able to perceive the appearance of God. These are not Kings Who Rule, but the Humble Man Who Works. These two streams are represented in Solomon and Hiram.

Solomon is the priest-king, the wisdom initiate. Hiram, as Solomon's architectural executive ,is able to master earthly forces and substances and so is able to build the Temple as Solomon with his wisdom is not able to do. There is a moment of greatest distress, when Solomon and Hiram misunderstand one another. (Solomon is not completely purified, and is jealous of Hiram.) It is the moment when Hiram wants to melt the metals, uniting them for the brazen sea. It is the moment of trying to unite the two streams. Solomon fails, and Hiram, in spiritual vision is removed to the center of the earth, where he experiences Cain, the representative of murderers, cast out of Paradise. Hiram has a certain initiation; it shows him, through Cain, into the cosmic past and future of man.

One of the most remarkable moments in the occult history of humanity is given in the Legend of the Temple. Hiram leads our spiritual vision back to Cain. Solomon also leads our spiritual vision back—and we are faced with the problem of Abel and Cain, the problem at the basis of the relationship of human beings with one another and of the relationship of human beings to God.

In all humility, I say: It has always puzzled me why Jahve accepted the incense of Abel and did not accept that of Cain, the farmer who worked hard. His offer of a sacrifice was refused. Abel, the herdsman, did much less work, and is the prototype of the hunter who takes away from nature. This story always revolts me. Why? And why is it the worker who loses his temper and perishes as a murderer?

But if we look at it from a deeper point of view we might understand it better. Jahve is one of the six Elohim. Five are on the Sun, directly under the Sun God. These five are representative of the wisdom whose latest descendant is the human intellect. Jahve is on the moon sphere, the sphere of pure wisdom that produced the body of human beings and of the earth and also nature. It is understandable when we consider Jahve, who lives in that Wisdom which produced nature, our physical nature and powers of reproduction, etc. It is Abel who collects the fruits of growth and reproduction and collects them in an unspoiled way. He collects what Jahve created and brings it back in sacrifice to Jahve. He, so to say, returns to Jahve the Jahve Creation, and Jahve likes that. Whereas Cain has changed, has worked on the world of Jahve and added human matter to it. He has spoiled the Creation of Jahve and replaced it with a man-made world. Jahve has to refuse it. Other gods, had they been worshipped, might have accepted Cain's sacrifice, but it was fate that Jahve refused it, and the forces of temper and destruction entered the human soul.

This was necessary, because the human soul needed to develop freedom. It was given to Cain to create a man-made world.

We see the King Stream, beloved of Jahve, continue; and we see how the outcast stream, dwelling in the world marked with the sign of Cain, had to continue to purify itself and develop freedom, the inner maturity of the soul which does not destroy, does not kill any longer. In the continuation of this development we see the spiritual stream which was the immediate predecessor of the shepherds, we see the stream of the Buddha. In Buddha, the human being is so purified that one no longer bears the sign of Cain. This being was so purified, through developing Manas, Buddhi and Atma, that he could dissolve the body when he entered the Buddha state. He no longer had the necessity of creating karma, so he had no need of reincarnation. He ascended out of the realm of Cain to the final, spiritual state. The Shepherds, the adoring human souls were pupils of Buddha, able to conquer the destructive forces of the soul, and able to see first a vision of the Sun God and then the real Sun God. In the Shepherds are found the lowest and the highest in the state in the stream of Cain and Hiram.

The descending path of the Sun God—Christ—to earth is pictured in the ancient Mysteries. The Sun God was worshipped as a Nature Phenomenon (an outer phenomenon) in the Eastern as well as the Western Mysteries. We find in the Druidic Mysteries of Celtic origin (in Western France, Normandy and Wales) that the death and birth of the Sun God was celebrated yearly at the Winter Solstice. The temples are crude physically, but built with astronomical wisdom. The dolmans accurately mark the lowest point of the sun and its return. It is a peculiar thing that at no time did it occur to the Druids that the sun would revive again out of itself. Each year they prayed to the Cosmos that the sun would revive and rise again. We take this for granted today; to the Druids it was a matter of worship and prayer. The Druids celebrated the Winter Solstice probably already 10,000 years before Christ. The Druid priest, praying in the artificial cave under the dolmen stone observed the disc of the sun go to its lowest point. Then he had a vision of a bird bringing the form of a child and the new sun was experienced as a child form at that moment of the Winter Solstice.

It is a peculiar situation in the Mysteries that all those of cosmic orientation have twelve zodiacal signs, and all those of inner soul-development have signs numbering seven—connected with the seven planetary forces. The Druidic Mysteries celebrated the Sun through the Zodiac and its twelve signs. The Mysteries of the East, the Buddha Mysteries of the development of inner soul forces, were based on inner experience of the seven planetary forces, the seven metal forces. These two streams, of the Shepherds and Kings, of Abel and

Cain, opposed each other up to the Mystery of Golgotha. They were not living in peace, they did not understand each other. And they did not even come in contact at the moment of the Birth of Christ. The Shepherds and the Kings were still two streams.

Out of the Shepherds developed the esoteric Christian stream of the Holy Grail. The first bearers of the Grail developed out of the Arthurian Round Table, which grew out of the Druidic Mysteries. Out of the twelve signs of the Zodiac they came, through the Grail worship to worship of that which transforms the inner soul forces. This transformation of the twelvefold of the Zodiac to the sevenfold of what lives in the inner soul was a step accomplished through the Initiation of the Holy Grail. The knights developed the seven virtues—later the basis of Scholasticism—not as thought forces but through actually living them. The knights did not *think* the seven virtues, they *acted* them. When the Knights of Arthur took over the Grail, they took over what had been prepared by Buddha and the Shepherds. This (which is difficult to put into words) takes place as a kind of cross in the history of the Mysteries. Those devoted to the inner life as Buddha pupils become Knights of Artis. The souls of "inner peace" change over to outer activity as knights and kings. The soul can only experience this by going through the state of the Shepherds.

The Kings also, on the other side, transform, lose their kinghood, their traditional attitude of connection with the cosmic wisdom. They also become earthly, and become kings of thoughts, not outer kings; they are represented as such in the School of Chartres and other mystery schools. From worship of the cosmos, they come to experience inner forces of the soul, an impulse which they could not only know but do something with. Those who have given up the rulership become humble human beings who, in thought, have to create again, in thought, the cosmos. The Sun God has entered Nature and the earth, and the human soul now has to do this task so that the Sun God can be experienced from within. St. Paul is one of those who has seen and experienced this.

History is a demonstration of a continuous process in which these two streams first fight each other, then cross each other, and then unite. These two streams of the inner and outer aspect live in every human being. Cain and Abel are parts of every single human being. We carry both of these forces within ourselves, and according to our Karma and status, we are representatives of one or the other stream.

So, in spiritual movements based on the Mysteries, we will find these two streams. We will see that in the past they fought to the death. But if we understand the Christmas Mystery, the Birth of the Sun God, we will be able to overcome the forces of the Kings and Shepherds and create a new entity. *The Philosophy of Spiritual Activity* and Anthroposophy are a step to bringing the two streams together. Humanity has to achieve freedom, because this union can only come into being out of freedom. It cannot be forced or taught, but can only be *done*. From *The Philosophy of Spiritual Activity* we learn to live in the love of an action, and at the same time to understand the volition of another person.

From the standpoint of morality, freedom is the last stage in humanity's evolution. And Dr. Steiner speaks of the power of love, which can only be perceived and used if people reach the stage of true freedom. People used to say that love is blind; it is no longer blind. That of which he speaks is the Spirit of Divine Love which incorporated in the Jesus Child born in Bethlehem. It is the power which can enable human beings to unite the forces of Abel and Cain, of the Kings and the Shepherds. This Divine Love is not given, but can be acquired. People have to achieve freedom so they can grasp this fruit. Christ cannot force Himself on humanity, even though He sacrificed Himself for humanity. This is true to the concept of Freedom, and true to His mission. It appears that one should really see Christ to recognize Him. It was put before each Apostle that he should see and recognize Christ. To recognize Christ, this is the important question.

The organ by which we recognize Christ is an organ that develops in the soul as a spiritual sense organ, deeper and farther reaching than any others. As we have physical organs for perceiving light and sound, we have organs of the spirit that can be developed and used. But the organ to perceive Christ, to see Him face to face has to be developed out of freedom, in every individual human soul.

In the *Mystery Dramas*, we find this described in the first play, *The Portal of Initiation*. The seeress, Theodora, is a soul developed to purity, simpleness and humbleness, out of the Buddha-Shepherd Stream. She says:

> "I am impelled to speak,
> Before my spirit stands a form in shining light"...

Her words reflect the development of a new sense, for being able to see Christ. This development of the new sense organ to perceive the Christ stands, probably, in the center of Rudolf Steiner's teaching. If we understand anthroposophy rightly, so that we not only think and read it but, like the Grail Knights, engage in *doing*, if we experience *The Philosophy of Spiritual Activity*, then we will develop spiritual organs—more or less successfully according to the extent to which our karma permits us—and one day we will develop the highest organ, the organ for perceiving Christ.

This organ is embedded in every human being, since the Mystery of Golgotha. It will, in the future, change the physical heart, so that the organ will find its center and projection through the physical heart. Thomas Aquinas pondered on this problem without reaching the solution. Rudolf Steiner discovered the transference of the etheric streams to the heart center. This organ exists in the etheric heart, but it also projects itself into the physical. Many human beings today are called upon to develop this organ. Probably the tremendous increase in heart disease at this time comes about because human beings sin against the heart instead of developing it.

The spiritual organ for perceiving the Christ is fostered and protected by a spiritual being that goes with us on our path through the earth. Zarathustra called him the Guardian, also the Companion. Manes called him the Companion. This Being will be made known to us in one way or another. To understand this Guardian-Companion we can turn to the Mystery Plays. Philia, Astrid, and Luna are the representatives of the three soul forces. They are also the three friends of Maria.

It is a super-imposing of two realms. These three exist within every human soul. We all carry in us, thought, feeling, and will—devotion, love and wisdom. Also, we can meet them outwardly, because one human being, throughout life, has developed one or another of these in an intensive way. So we meet one and another of them as human beings, as in the Plays they appear as friends of Maria. We meet these soul forces as our own. And also we meet them in another human being if we develop what Dr. Steiner described as that love which is not blind but which opens the eyes to the better forces in the other being. If we experience these three in our own being, then we look on the other human being with that greater love projected into our self by the Guardian-Companion. Then we can see Philia, Asrid and Luna accompanying the other person, and our own Philia, Asrid and Luna can communicate with the Philia, Astrid and Luna accompanying the other one. This is a reality which can be experienced.

The Companion undergoes suffering because he has to walk with us on our earthly path of errors and trials, until one day we are able to unite with him. He goes with us in order to revive the two streams within our souls. He leads us to a Higher Being, makes active our eye for the perception of Christ. This Higher Being is mentioned in *The Apocalypse* as the Woman Clothed with the Sun. (Here the speaker read relevant passages from *The Book of Revelation*.)

This Imagination of the Woman Clothed with the Sun who is in childbirth, is a peculiar one, because in all traditional and present occultism, a woman in childbirth is always clothed with moon forces. But the fact is that the moon forces, through the action of Christ, are transformed again. The forces of reproduction are taken away from the moon and restored to the sun. The moon forces of reproduction reproduce their own kind—out of the seed of a rose, a rose grows; out of the ovum and sperm of the animal, the same kind of animal grows. The seed of the moon repeats itself, so also in human beings.

These forces are transformed into sun forces. Jahve returns to the other Elohim on the Sun. Actually, as Rudolf Steiner has said, the moon will, however, not return to the Sun but will unite with the earth. This is because the Cosmic Spirit of the Sun united, in Christ, with the earth. So Jahve, in the far future, unites, not with the Sun, but casts himself on the earth. This is the beginning of the New Creation, the New Sun, the Woman Clothed with the Sun, who is attacked by the dragon and defended by Michael and the angels.

This is the spiritual future; and the Companion is leading the soul to understand the future. In the future, the creative forces, under the guidance of Christ, will act so that human beings can reproduce human beings, not on the basis of physical reproduction through the moon forces, but on the basis of what is actually called the Word of Logos. In the final end of humanity's development, a person will, under the guidance of Christ, reproduce the Spirit through the Logos. One will undo the harm that has been done by Cain and Abel, the Kings and the Shepherds, accomplishing this by uniting all the forces and leading them upwards.

The Companion, who can be perceived by awakened eyes, this Being, is at present a young being that can only be developed insofar as we perceive and act out of freedom. This Being is the one that Rudolf Steiner called Anthroposophy. Dr. Steiner said that Anthroposophy is at present an Angel Being, who as Companion approaches human souls and tries to lead them to the development of an organ for the perception of Christ. This is a Being created in the Spirit, through free human minds and individualities. This Being will grow to the extent to which the free human being perceives it.

The question facing us is whether we perish as Cain and Abel, die and disappear in matter, or whether we revive as spiritual beings carried into the realm of the Logos. The answer depends on our task with the Being, Anthroposophy, and on whether we develop our sense for Christ so that we see Christ face to face. This is the future task for which we have to prepare. On an ancient Christmas, God descended to earth to face human souls. On a future Christmas, human souls will ascend and stand before God, face to face.